J.R. HARRIS

Tax Lien Investing

Real Estate Success with Little Money

First edition

This book was professionally typeset on Reedsy.
Find out more at reedsy.com

Contents

Introduction 1

   Tax Lien Investing: Real Estate Success

   with Little Money 1

     Introduction 1

Chapter 1: Understanding Tax Liens and Tax Deeds 2

     1.1 What Are Tax Liens? 2

     1.2 What Are Tax Deeds? 2

     1.3 Key Differences Between Tax Liens

        and Tax Deeds 3

Chapter 2: Why Choose Tax Liens Over Tax Deeds 4

     2.1 Lower Investment Requirement 4

     2.2 Steady Returns with Less Risk 4

     2.3 Simplicity and Ease of Management 5

     2.4 Legal Protections 5

Chapter 3: Getting Started with Tax Lien Investing 7

     3.1 Researching State and Local Laws 7

     3.2 Identifying Reputable Online Platforms 7

     3.3 Setting Your Investment Budget 8

     3.4 Analyzing Tax Lien Properties 8

Chapter 4: Bidding on Tax Liens 9

     4.1 Participating in Online Auctions 9

     4.2 Winning the Bid 9

     4.3 Managing Your Tax Lien Portfolio 10

Chapter 5: Collecting Returns and Foreclosure 11

5.1 Collecting Interest Payments   11

5.2 Foreclosure Process   11

5.3 Acquiring Property Through Foreclosure   12

Chapter 6: Case Studies and Success Stories   13

6.1 Case Study 1: Small Investment, Big Returns   13

6.2 Case Study 2: From Tax Lien to
Property Ownership   14

6.3 Case Study 3: Consistent Returns
Through Diversification   16

Chapter 7: Tips and Best Practices for Tax
Lien Investing   18

7.1 Diversifying Your Investments   18

7.2 Staying Informed and Updated   18

7.3 Building a Network   19

Conclusion   19

Appendix: Resources and References   20

Appendix: Resources and References   20

HELPFUL LINKS: 21

Introduction

Tax Lien Investing: Real Estate Success with Little Money

Introduction

Real estate investing can often seem like an exclusive club reserved for those with deep pockets. However, with the right strategy, even individuals with limited funds can successfully dive into the real estate market. One such strategy involves buying tax liens online. This Book will provide a comprehensive guide on how you can start investing in real estate through tax liens, the differences between tax liens and tax deeds, and why choosing tax liens can be a strategic decision for novice investors.

Chapter 1: Understanding Tax Liens and Tax Deeds

1.1 What Are Tax Liens?

A tax lien is a legal claim by a government entity against a property when the property owner fails to pay property taxes. The government entity sells these liens to investors to recoup the unpaid taxes. As an investor, you purchase the lien and gain the right to collect the unpaid taxes plus interest from the property owner.

Key Points:

- **Legal Claim:** A lien is not ownership but a claim.
- **Interest Earnings:** Investors earn interest on unpaid taxes.
- **Redemption Period:** Property owners can pay back the debt within a certain period.

1.2 What Are Tax Deeds?

A tax deed represents ownership of the property itself. When property taxes go unpaid, the government entity may sell the property at a tax deed auction to recover the unpaid taxes. The highest bidder at the auction receives the deed to the property, essentially becoming the new owner.

Key Points:

- **Immediate Ownership:** The highest bidder becomes the owner.
- **No Redemption:** Once sold, the property doesn't go back to the original owner.
- **Higher Risk:** You assume all responsibilities of property ownership.

1.3 Key Differences Between Tax Liens and Tax Deeds

- **Ownership vs. Claim:** A tax lien gives you a claim on the property and the right to collect unpaid taxes with interest, while a tax deed gives you ownership of the property.
- **Risk Level:** Tax liens typically involve less risk compared to tax deeds. With tax liens, you earn interest on your investment regardless of the property's condition. With tax deeds, you assume ownership and all responsibilities associated with the property.
- **Redemption Period:** Tax liens often come with a redemption period during which the property owner can repay the taxes and interest to reclaim their property. Tax deeds generally result in immediate ownership transfer.

Chapter 2: Why Choose Tax Liens Over Tax Deeds

2.1 Lower Investment Requirement

Tax lien investments typically require less upfront capital compared to tax deeds. You are investing in the unpaid taxes, not the property's market value. This makes tax liens an accessible entry point for investors with limited funds.

Examples:

- **Smaller Outlay:** Instead of thousands, you might need only a few hundred dollars.
- **Incremental Growth:** Start small and gradually increase your investments.

2.2 Steady Returns with Less Risk

Investing in tax liens can offer steady returns with lower risk. When you purchase a tax lien, you are entitled to collect the unpaid taxes plus interest, which is often higher than standard investment returns. If the property owner redeems the lien, you earn the interest. If not, you may eventually acquire the property

at a significant discount.
Details:

- **Interest Rates:** Typically range from 8% to 36%.
- **Redemption:** Most owners redeem their property, securing your interest earnings.
- **Foreclosure Option:** If unredeemed, you can foreclose and acquire the property.

2.3 Simplicity and Ease of Management

Tax liens are relatively straightforward to manage. Unlike property ownership, you don't have to deal with tenant issues, property maintenance, or other responsibilities that come with owning real estate. Your primary task is to wait for the property owner to redeem the lien or to initiate foreclosure proceedings if they do not.
Advantages:

- **Minimal Hassle:** No need to worry about repairs or tenants.
- **Administrative Focus:** Your main task is tracking lien statuses and managing paperwork.

2.4 Legal Protections

Tax lien investments are often backed by state laws that protect your investment. If the property owner fails to pay, you may have the legal right to foreclose and acquire the property. This legal backing adds a layer of security to your investment.
Security Factors:

- **Statutory Protections:** States provide legal frameworks protecting lien holders.
- **Due Process:** Legal processes ensure fair treatment and security.

Chapter 3: Getting Started with Tax Lien Investing

3.1 Researching State and Local Laws

Tax lien and tax deed laws vary by state and locality. It is crucial to understand the specific regulations governing tax lien sales in your target area. Some states favor tax liens, while others may offer more tax deed sales. Here are some helpful resources:

- National Tax Lien Association
- Investopedia – Tax Lien Definition

3.2 Identifying Reputable Online Platforms

Several online platforms facilitate tax lien sales. These platforms provide access to tax lien auctions from various jurisdictions. Reputable platforms often offer detailed property information, auction schedules, and customer support to guide you through the process. Some popular platforms include:

- Bid4Assets
- RealAuction

- GovEase

3.3 Setting Your Investment Budget

Determine how much you are willing to invest in tax liens. Start with a modest amount to gain experience and gradually increase your investment as you become more comfortable with the process.

3.4 Analyzing Tax Lien Properties

Before bidding on a tax lien, thoroughly research the property. Consider factors such as location, property value, and the amount of unpaid taxes. Online platforms typically provide property information and tax history, which can aid your decision-making.

Research Tips:

- **Location Matters:** Higher value areas can be more stable.
- **Debt vs. Value:** Ensure the unpaid taxes are a small fraction of the property value.
- **Property Condition:** Understand the property's state even though you're buying the debt.

Chapter 4: Bidding on Tax Liens

4.1 Participating in Online Auctions

Most tax lien auctions are conducted online, allowing you to participate from the comfort of your home. Register on your chosen platform, review available liens, and place your bids. Pay attention to auction schedules and deadlines.

Auction Tips:

- **Timing:** Bids often come in at the last minute; stay vigilant.
- **Budget Discipline:** Set and stick to a maximum bid.

4.2 Winning the Bid

If you win the bid, you must pay the amount of the lien plus any auction fees. The government entity will then issue a tax lien certificate to you, officially making you the lien holder.

Next Steps:

- **Certificate Issuance:** Ensure you receive and store the certificate securely.
- **Payment Methods:** Be prepared to pay immediately after

winning.

4.3 Managing Your Tax Lien Portfolio

Once you acquire tax liens, keep track of their status. Monitor redemption periods, property owner payments, and any legal actions required to protect your investment.

Management Tools:

- **Spreadsheet Tracking:** Use tools like Excel or Google Sheets.
- **Alerts and Reminders:** Set calendar alerts for key dates and deadlines.

Chapter 5: Collecting Returns and Foreclosure

5.1 Collecting Interest Payments

If the property owner redeems the lien, you will receive the unpaid taxes plus interest. Ensure you have a process in place to collect these payments, whether through the online platform or directly from the government entity.

Collection Tips:

- **Verification:** Always verify payment amounts and dates.
- **Documentation:** Keep records of all transactions.

5.2 Foreclosure Process

If the property owner fails to redeem the lien within the redemption period, you may initiate foreclosure proceedings to acquire the property. This process varies by jurisdiction, so understanding local foreclosure laws is essential. Useful resources include:

- Nolo – Tax Lien Foreclosure

Foreclosure Steps:

- **Legal Advice:** Consult with a real estate attorney.
- **Due Diligence:** Ensure all notices and legal requirements are met.

5.3 Acquiring Property Through Foreclosure

Successfully foreclosing on a property transfers ownership to you. While this is a potential outcome of tax lien investing, it is not the primary goal. Most investors prefer to earn interest on their liens rather than acquire property.

Considerations:

- **Property Condition:** Be prepared for potential rehabilitation costs.
- **Exit Strategy:** Plan how you will manage or sell the property.

Chapter 6: Case Studies and Success Stories

6.1 Case Study 1: Small Investment, Big Returns

Background:

John, a middle-aged office worker with limited savings, decided to explore tax lien investing as a way to grow his wealth. With only $1,000 to start, he was cautious but determined.

Strategy:

John researched extensively, learning about tax lien laws in his state and identifying reputable online platforms. He began by purchasing small liens in well-populated counties with a history of high redemption rates.

Process:

1. **Research:** John focused on properties in stable neighborhoods with good resale value.
2. **Auction Participation:** He participated in several online auctions, winning liens on properties with a total unpaid tax of $800, leaving him with a small reserve for fees.
3. **Management:** John kept meticulous records and monitored the redemption periods closely.

Outcome:

- **Interest Earned:** Within a year, 80% of the property owners redeemed their liens, and John earned an average interest of 12%, netting him a profit of $96.
- **Reinvestment:** John reinvested his returns and initial capital into more liens, gradually increasing his portfolio.

Lessons Learned:

- **Start Small:** Begin with manageable investments to build experience.
- **Thorough Research:** Understanding local laws and property conditions is crucial.
- **Patience:** Returns might take time, but consistent reinvestment can compound growth.

6.2 Case Study 2: From Tax Lien to Property Ownership

Background:

Sarah, an experienced real estate investor, saw an opportunity in tax lien investing to diversify her portfolio. With a budget of $10,000, she aimed to acquire properties through foreclosure.

Strategy:

Sarah targeted high-value properties with significant unpaid taxes, assuming higher risk for potentially greater rewards. She focused on areas with high foreclosure rates and did detailed property evaluations.

Process:

1. **Targeted Research:** Sarah identified properties in up-and-

coming neighborhoods with a high chance of redevelopment.

2. **Auction Participation:** She won several high-value liens, with individual liens ranging from $2,000 to $4,000.
3. **Due Diligence:** Sarah ensured all her liens were on properties with clear titles and no other significant liens.

Outcome:

- **Foreclosure:** One of the property owners failed to redeem the lien within the redemption period. Sarah initiated foreclosure proceedings and acquired a property worth $150,000 for just $4,000.
- **Renovation:** She invested an additional $20,000 into renovating the property.
- **Sale:** Sarah sold the property for $200,000, netting a substantial profit.

Lessons Learned:

- **Higher Risk, Higher Reward:** Targeting higher-value properties can lead to significant returns.
- **Due Diligence is Critical:** Ensuring clear titles and understanding property conditions are essential to avoid legal issues.
- **Exit Strategy:** Having a clear plan for property management or sale is vital.

6.3 Case Study 3: Consistent Returns Through Diversification

Background:

Mike, a retired teacher, wanted to supplement his pension through safe, consistent investments. With a budget of $5,000, he aimed for a diverse tax lien portfolio.

Strategy:

Mike diversified his investments across several states to spread risk and increase the chances of lien redemption.

Process:

1. **Diverse Investments:** Mike invested in tax liens in multiple states, each with different interest rates and redemption periods.
2. **Online Tools:** He used online platforms to manage his portfolio, ensuring timely payments and monitoring redemption statuses.
3. **Regular Reinvestment:** Mike reinvested his returns into new liens, gradually growing his portfolio.

Outcome:

- **Steady Income:** Mike earned an average annual return of 10%, adding $500 to his pension each year.
- **Low Risk:** Diversification helped mitigate risks associated with non-redeemed liens.

Lessons Learned:

- **Diversification:** Spreading investments across various locations reduces risk.

- **Consistent Reinvestment:** Regularly reinvesting returns can compound growth over time.
- **Technology Utilization:** Using online tools for management can streamline the process and reduce oversight risks.

Chapter 7: Tips and Best Practices for Tax Lien Investing

7.1 Diversifying Your Investments

Spread your investments across multiple tax liens to mitigate risk. Diversification can protect your portfolio from the impact of a single lien failing to redeem.
   Strategies:

- **Geographic Spread:** Invest in multiple states or counties.
- **Lien Sizes:** Mix smaller and larger liens to balance risk and reward.

7.2 Staying Informed and Updated

Keep abreast of changes in tax lien laws, market conditions, and auction schedules. Staying informed allows you to adapt your strategies and make informed investment decisions. Some valuable resources include:

- National Association of Counties
- PropertyRadar Blog

Staying Updated:

- **Newsletters:** Subscribe to relevant industry newsletters.
- **Forums:** Join online forums and groups for tax lien investors.

7.3 Building a Network

Connect with other tax lien investors, real estate professionals, and legal experts. Networking can provide valuable insights, support, and opportunities for collaboration.

Networking Tips:

- **Local Meetups:** Attend local real estate investment groups.
- **Online Communities:** Engage in online communities like BiggerPockets.

Conclusion

Tax lien investing offers a viable path into real estate for those with limited funds. By understanding the nuances of tax liens and tax deeds, conducting thorough research, and leveraging online platforms, you can start building a profitable investment portfolio. With lower risks and the potential for steady returns, tax liens present an attractive option for novice investors seeking to enter the real estate market with little to no money.

Appendix: Resources and References

Appendix: Resources and References

- **Online Tax Lien Auction Platforms:**
- Bid4Assets
- RealAuction
- GovEase
- **State and Local Government Resources:** Links to government websites with information on tax lien and tax deed sales.
- **Further Reading:**
- National Tax Lien Association
- Investopedia - Tax Lien Definition
- Nolo - Tax Lien Foreclosure

This Book aims to equip you with the knowledge and confidence to start your journey in real estate investing through tax liens. Remember, success in this field requires patience, diligence, and continuous learning. Happy investing!

HELPFUL LINKS:

Refresh.Goddelyke.com
Iq.Goddelyke.com
Dispute.Goddelyke.com
Grow.Goddelyke.com

www.ingramcontent.com/pod-product-compliance
Lightning Source LLC
Chambersburg PA
CBHW070443240526
45479CB00013B/343